ENGINEERING EVOLUTIONS

Harnessing Energy

From Powering the Past to Creating a Cleaner Future

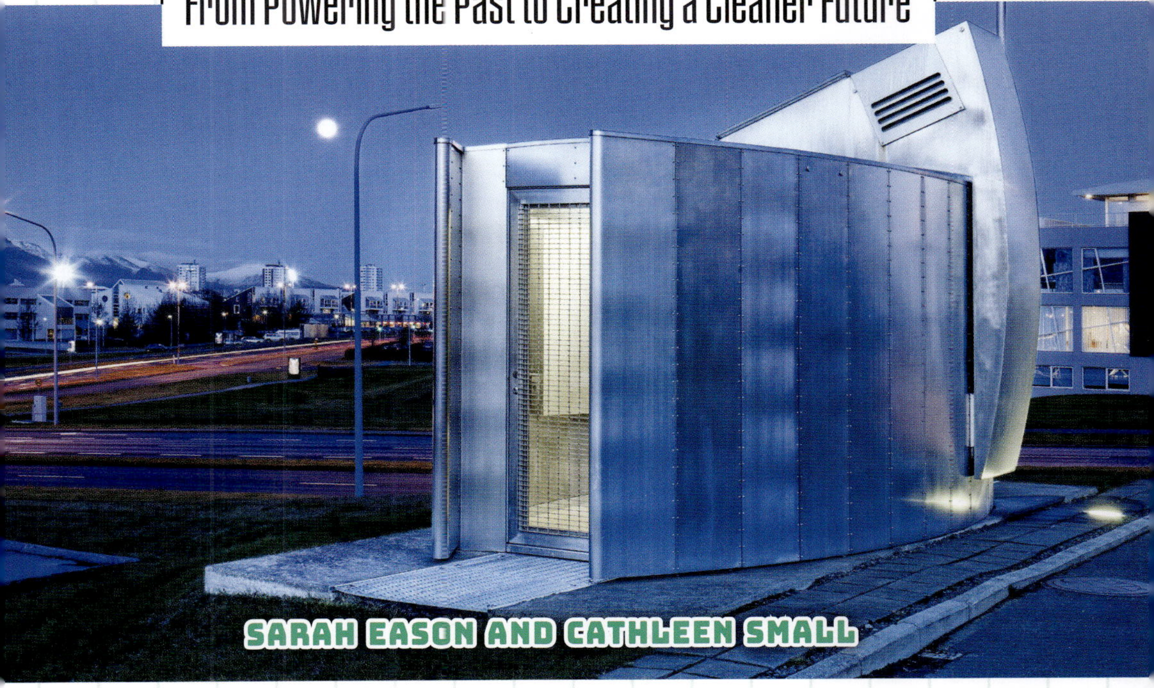

SARAH EASON AND CATHLEEN SMALL

Published in 2026 by Cheriton Children's Books
1 Bank Drive West, Shrewsbury, Shropshire, SY3 9DJ, UK

First Edition

Authors: Sarah Eason and Cathleen Small
Editor: Jennifer Sanderson
Designer: Paul Myerscough
Proofreader: Ellie Truman

Picture credits: Cover: Shutterstock/Pavel Chlum (left), Shutterstock/OKAWA PHOTO (right). Inside: p1: Shutterstock/Cavan Images, p4: Wikimedia Commons/RM VM, p5: Shutterstock/Hryshchyshen Serhii, p6: Shutterstock/Gorodenkoff, p7: Shutterstock/Gorodenkoff, p8: Shutterstock/Best View Stock, p9: Shutterstock/Vova Shevchuk, p10: Shutterstock/JossK, p11: Shutterstock/AlpKaya, p12: Shutterstock/AI Generator, p13: Shutterstock/Veroniksha, p14: Shutterstock/Mihai Andritoiu, p15: Shutterstock/DimaSid, p16: Shutterstock/Maxshot.pl, p17: Shutterstock/Yulia B, p18: Shutterstock/Joseph Creamer, p19: Shutterstock/PradeepGaurs, p20: Shutterstock/IM Imagery, p21: Shutterstock/Marc Bode, p22: Shutterstock/Graphixmania, p23: Shutterstock/Pradeep Gaurs, p24: Shutterstock/Eakarat Buanoi, p25: Shutterstock/Mariana Serdynska, p26: Shutterstock/Arnav Pratap Singh, p27: Wikimedia Commons/UC Davis College of Engineering, p28: Shutterstock/Vladimka Production, p29: Shutterstock/Javier Jaime, p30: Shutterstock/Esbobeldijk, p31: Shutterstock/Fokke Baarssen, p32: Shutterstock/R Classen, p33: Shutterstock/Jacques Tarnero, p34: Shutterstock/Frans Blok, p35: Wikimedia Commons/Equinor ASA, p36: U.S. National Science Foundation, p36r: Wikimedia Commons/Olivierabristol, p37: Shutterstock/TTstudio, p38: Shutterstock/Tupungato, p39: Shutterstock/Burakyalcin, p41: Shutterstock/Ethan Daniels, p41: Shutterstock/Alex Mit, p42: Shutterstock/Zacarias da Mata, p43: Shutterstock/Phillip B. Espinasse, p44: Shutterstock/FoxGrafy, p45: Shutterstock/Weniliou, p46: Shutterstock/Cybercrisi, p47: Shutterstock/Cavan Images, p48: Shutterstock/Pavel Svoboda Photography, p49: Shutterstock/Pi Lens, p50: Shutterstock/The Desert Photo, p51: Flickr/U.S. Department of State, p52: Shutterstock/Studio Harmony, p53: Shutterstock/Danielsen Photography, p54: Wikimedia Commons/Johannes Reimer, p55: Wikimedia Commons/National Renewable Energy Laboratory/Dennis Schroeder, p56: Shutterstock/Gorodenkoff, p57: Shutterstock/Gorodenkoff, p58: Shutterstock/Halfpoint, p59: Shutterstock/Wut Anunai.

Printed in China

Please visit our website,
www.cheritonchildrensbooks.com
to see more of our high-quality books.

CONTENTS

EVOLUTIONS IN ENGINEERING

Engineering is the use of scientific, mathematical, and practical ideas to design and create things. Those things include buildings, machines, devices, and systems that solve problems and improve people's lives. Engineers are people who come up with the ideas for those solutions. They have invented incredible ways to help people source energy throughout the ages. From the creation of tools to make fire in early human history through the Industrial Revolution and the generation of energy on a grand scale, great engineering minds have found ever-evolving ways to provide us with the energy we need to survive.

What Is Energy?

Energy is the ability to do work and power things. Through the years, engineers have found ways to change energy from one form to another, and then use it to do work. To date, people have mainly used energy from coal, oil, and natural gas, which are fossil fuels that are burned for power. We use that power to create electricity to light our buildings and make machinery work. We also use it to make our vehicles move along roads, across water, and through the sky.

Problems with Energy Use

More than half of the energy the world uses comes from burning fossil fuels in power plants. Fossil fuels are in limited supply—it took millions of years for them to form so we cannot easily replace them. For that reason, these sources of power are called nonrenewable. The other problem with using fossil fuels is that burning them to make electricity creates harmful gases that trap heat from the sun and warm Earth's atmosphere. This is causing changes to the global climate, which has a dangerous effect on our planet.

Engineering Past, Present, and Future

Today we face greater challenges than ever in our quest for energy. Scientists are warning us that we need to reduce our reliance on fossil fuels and instead try to use renewable forms of energy, such as solar power, wind power, water power, and geothermal power. The challenge for engineers is to find ever-more inventive and efficient ways of harnessing and distributing these sources of power. Can the engineers of today and tomorrow find solutions to these big challenges?

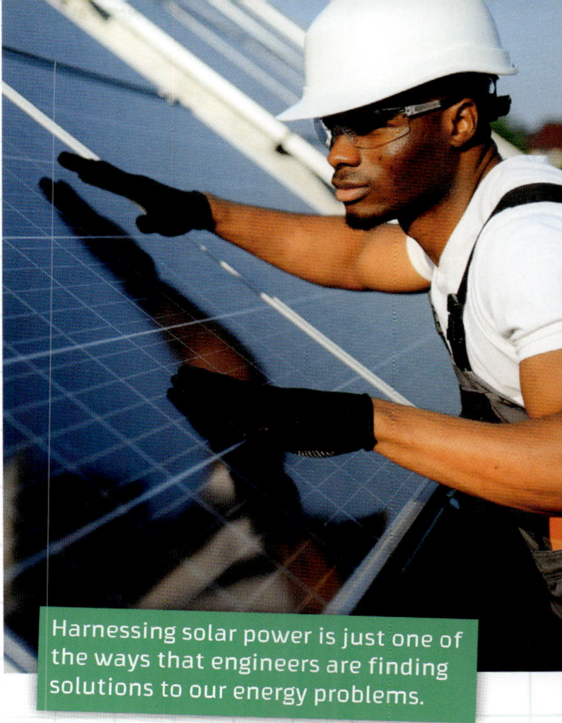

Harnessing solar power is just one of the ways that engineers are finding solutions to our energy problems.

Burning fossil fuels is harmful for our planet. We need to find better ways to power our world.

An Engineering Evolution

In this book, we'll explore great feats of energy engineering through history, from earliest times to the present day. We'll discover how engineering has evolved and how ancient engineering has inspired modern engineering. We'll learn how engineers have come up with resourceful ways to solve our current energy issues and how we have come full circle in this quest, harnessing renewable energy as ancient people did. We'll also explore the exciting developments in engineering that are just around the corner for the energy industry, and discover how they could provide the answer to our future energy needs.

CHAPTER 1

THE HISTORY OF ENERGY AND ENGINEERING

Engineering to source energy began in earliest times. Burning wood for fires was the first use of energy, and using tools to create fire is perhaps the most important energy engineering of all time. Making fires allowed people to cook food, rather than eating it raw. That helped kill parasites that could cause sickness and it also made food easier to digest. Being able to make fire as needed also allowed people to create light, so they could more easily find their way around in the dark. Fire was used as protection against dangerous animals in primitive times—fire is threatening to many animals and they avoid it.

BIG Breakthroughs

The creation of fire allowed for social gatherings. Around fires, ideas could be exchanged and bonds formed within communities. This human exchange of ideas is responsible for our development and the formation of civilization. It paved the way for future inventions in engineering to be shared among communities and then the wider world.

The ability to make fires transformed the way early humans lived.

The bow method of a fire drill

HOW IT WORKS:

MAKING A FIRE

Early humans learned to make fires using a variety of tools and technology, including:

Fire plough: This is the simplest way to make fire. It consists of a stick (the plough), which is rubbed against a groove in a piece of wood. The friction between the stick and groove creates heat, which eventually produces a small ember. That ember can then be transferred to a tinder bundle to start a fire.

Fire drill: In this method, a straight, slim stick (a spindle) is placed in a notch in a flat piece of wood (a fireboard). The stick is then spun by rubbing it between the palms of the hands. That friction creates heat and an ember. This method could also be more advanced, using a bow, spindle, and fireboard. The bow was wrapped around the spindle and pulled back and forth. That caused the spindle to spin against the fireboard, creating heat.

Fire saw: This method involves sawing a piece of wood against another to create heat through friction.

Fire thong: Here, a strip of flexible material, such as leather or plant fiber, is looped around a stick. This thong is then pulled back and forth to spin the stick against a piece of wood, creating friction, heat, and an ember.

Early Uses of Sun Energy

In ancient Greece, people made use of solar power, or the energy from the sun. They designed their buildings to capture the maximum amount of sunlight during the winter months to keep them warm. The Romans too used the energy of the sun to heat their buildings, designing their bathhouses with large south-facing windows that captured sunlight to heat the rooms inside. The ancient Chinese designed their buildings to capture as much sunlight as possible during the winter months to heat them. The buildings were also designed to minimize the amount of sunlight that entered buildings during the summer, keeping them cool.

ENGINEERING EVOLUTIONS

Discover how solar energy engineering has evolved from ancient times to today in Chapter 2.

Powered by Wind and Water

Early civilizations such as the ancient Egyptians (3100–30 BCE) and ancient Greeks (1100–146 BCE) learned how to use the power of wind and water. Using engineering to harness these two energy forms provided solutions to problems in both transportation and food creation. Ancient people invented sailboats to harness the energy of the wind to power their vessels across rivers and seas. They also discovered how to use water power by inventing water wheels and windmills. These devices powered mills in which grain was ground to make flour for bread and other foods.

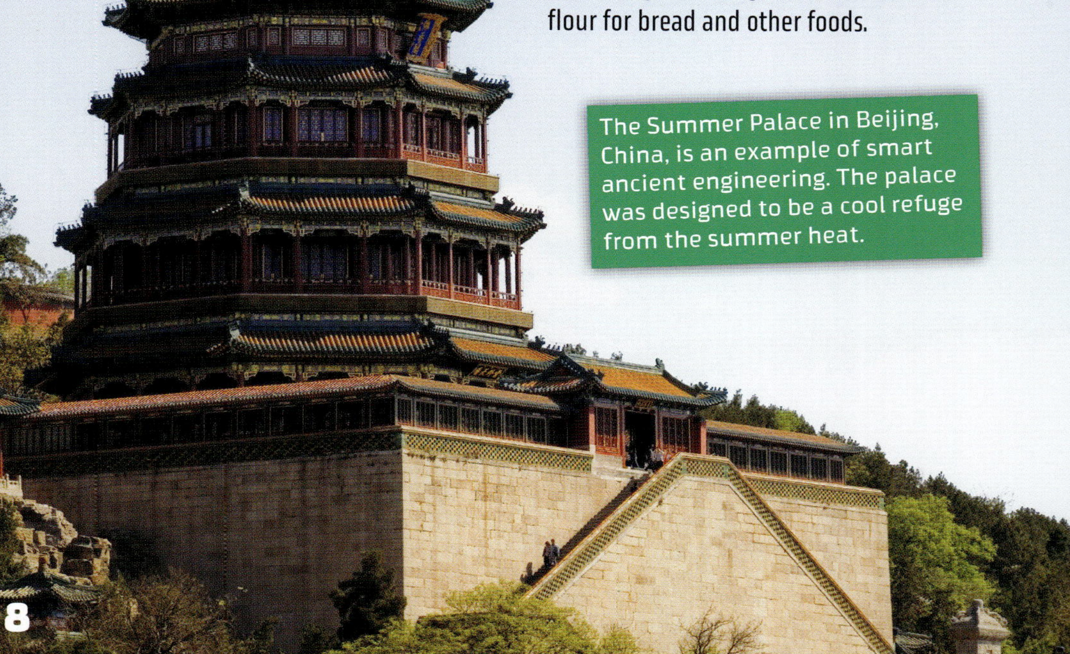

The Summer Palace in Beijing, China, is an example of smart ancient engineering. The palace was designed to be a cool refuge from the summer heat.

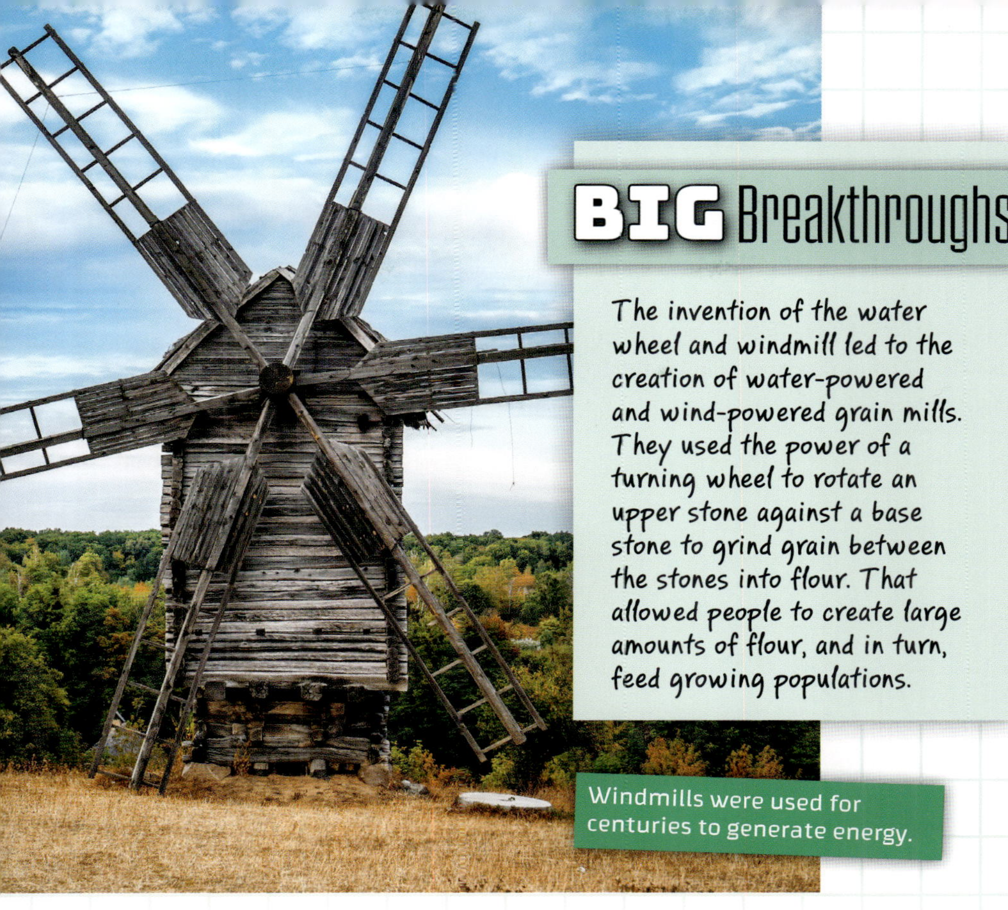

BIG Breakthroughs

The invention of the water wheel and windmill led to the creation of water-powered and wind-powered grain mills. They used the power of a turning wheel to rotate an upper stone against a base stone to grind grain between the stones into flour. That allowed people to create large amounts of flour, and in turn, feed growing populations.

Windmills were used for centuries to generate energy.

Early Water Wheels

The ancient Greeks were pioneers in using water power and are believed to have developed some of the earliest water wheels. These machines were simple vertical wheels over which water flowed, which rotated the wheel. The rotation converted kinetic energy from flowing water into mechanical energy. Later machines were more efficient, and could use either water that flowed beneath them or water that flowed over the top.

Ancient Windmills

The earliest known windmills appeared in Persia (modern-day Iran) around the seventh century CE. The blades of the mills were made from bundles of reeds or wood, and set in a circular pattern to capture the flow of wind. The wind turned the blades, which were linked to mechanical devices inside the mill, and in turn powered them.

ENGINEERING EVOLUTIONS

Learn how wind and water energy engineering has evolved from ancient times to today in Chapters 3 and 4. →

Engineering in Rome

During the time of the Roman Empire (27 BCE–476 CE) energy engineering leaped forward. One of the most famous engineering feats the Romans created was the hypocaust system. The hypocaust was an early form of central heating. The Romans used it in their public baths and villas, which were large houses that wealthy Romans lived in. The hypocaust system had an incredibly smart design. The floor of a building was raised on pillars to create space beneath. There, hot air from a furnace was circulated to heat the floors and walls of the building.

HOW IT WORKS:

HYPOCAUST AND MODERN CENTRAL HEATING

The hypocaust system influenced the development of modern central heating in several ways:

Radiant floor heating: The hypocaust system is an early form of radiant floor heating, where heat is distributed evenly across the floor surface. Modern radiant floor heating systems use electric cables or water-filled pipes installed beneath the floor to provide regular heat distribution.

Forced air circulation: The idea of circulating warm air from a central source, as used in the hypocaust, is also used in modern forced-air heating systems. Modern systems have ductwork to distribute heated air from a furnace to different parts of a building. That is similar to how the hypocaust circulated hot air under floors and through walls.

Efficient heating: The hypocaust provided even heating across large areas. Modern systems can also be adapted to control heating in different areas of a building.

The remains of a hypocaust system can be seen here.

The Romans also used naturally heated springs for their public baths.

BIG Breakthroughs

The Roman hypocaust system laid the groundwork for modern central heating. While technology has improved, the original ideas behind the hypocaust system are the basis for modern heating solutions.

ENGINEERING EVOLUTIONS

Learn how engineering using heat from inside Earth has evolved from ancient times to today in Chapter 5. →

Fast Forward to the Middle Ages

The Romans mainly burned wood to fuel the hypocaust system, and the use of wood as a source of energy continued for centuries after. However, there is evidence that people were mining coal during the time of the Romans. By the late Middle Ages (500–1500 CE), people were mining coal more intensively in Europe using engineering inventions.

Most coal was mined near the surface, where it was easy to reach. But some forms of underground mining also took place. Miners dug a vertical shaft to a coal seam, then dug outward from there, creating a round cavity shaped a little like a bell. This became known as a bell pit. The coal was dug out from the pit and transported to the surface. Miners also dug horizontal or slightly inclined tunnels in places where coal seams were exposed on hillsides. These were called drift mines.

Steaming Ahead with Engineering

Over the centuries that followed, the use of coal as an energy source developed further. By the seventeenth and eighteenth centuries, pioneering inventors like Thomas Newcomen (1663–1729) and James Watt (1736–1819) were using coal to create steam energy to power engines. Those steam engines were used to power factories, trains, and ships. That was a crucial moment in the Industrial Revolution and a forward charge into modern engineering in transportation.

Changing Life Forever

The Industrial Revolution is one of the most significant times in human engineering history. It paved the way for the rapid growth of industry and changed how people lived. New machines were built during the period, powered by advances in energy engineering. With the use of these powerful machines, goods could be created quickly and in large numbers. Those goods were then transported to where people needed them, carried by steam engines across vast networks of railroads. They were also transported across oceans by steam-powered ships.

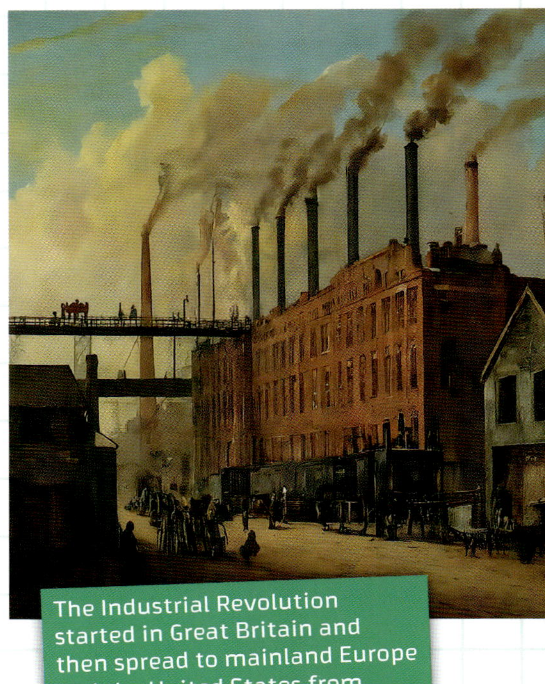

The Industrial Revolution started in Great Britain and then spread to mainland Europe and the United States from around 1760 to about 1840.

BIG Breakthroughs

The provision of electrical energy (see opposite) truly transformed the way people lived. It meant that people could use labor-saving devices such as refrigerators, washing machines, vacuum cleaners, and electric stoves. Streets were also lit at night using electric lights, as were homes and other buildings. Later, use of electricity would also mean that the sharing of information by radio and television became possible.

Power at the Touch of a Switch

By the nineteenth century, the brilliant minds of Thomas Edison (1847–1931) and Nikola Tesla (1856–1943) had further revolutionized the energy industry with their use of electricity. Both inventors developed systems that harnessed and distributed electrical energy, and power grids that would later feed that energy across countries began to take shape.

HOW IT WORKS: THE ELECTRICAL GRID

The electrical grid is a system that moves energy from where it is made to where it is needed. Here's how it works:

Made at power plants: Electricity is made at power plants using different energy sources. These can include burning fuels like coal or natural gas, or using renewable energy such as wind, sunlight, or water.

Sent along lines: Once generated, electricity is sent over high-voltage power lines. These special cables move electricity quickly across long distances.

To the substation: The electricity is sent to substations. Here, the voltage is adjusted.

Sent to where it is needed: Finally, the electricity travels through smaller power lines to homes, buildings, and factories.

An electrical substation distribution system transforms electricity into a lower-voltage form, which is safer to use.

This nuclear power plant is on the Hudson River, to the north of New York City.

Twentieth Century Evolutions

Into the twentieth century, engineering evolutions began to take place on a grand scale. The oil and gas industries grew quickly after World War II (1939–1945). Petroleum became the main source of fuel used for transportation, heating, and to power industrial processes. To provide the increasing demand for petroleum, offshore drilling began and oil refineries grew.

A New Power

After the war, another, new form of power was developed too: nuclear power. The discovery of this energy source partly came about with the development of the atomic bomb. The bomb harnessed atomic energy, which is created by a series of reactions that take place inside the nucleus, or center, of an atom. Nuclear power plants were developed in the 1950s, and began to create a lot of electricity that fed a growing demand for power.

The Issue of Nuclear Power

However, nuclear energy is considered a controversial form of energy by many people. Dealing with the radioactive waste that nuclear power plants create is difficult. There are also concerns around the safety of such power plants after disasters that have taken place at them. They include the Chernobyl Nuclear Power Plant in the former Soviet Union in 1986, and the near-disaster at the Fukushima Daiichi Nuclear Power Plant in 2011, which was caused when a tsunami hit Japan.

Twenty-First Century Problems

With the concerns about nuclear energy, many people are naturally worried about relying on it as a source of power. We are also now aware of the problems caused by burning fossil fuels. Over the last 70 years, we have used fossil fuels at an extraordinary rate. Scientists began to study the effect that burning fossil fuels has on Earth's atmosphere in the 1960s. Since then, the race to find engineering solutions to our growing need for clean energy has become a priority.

Twenty-First Century Solutions

Today, engineers are focused on creating sustainable, safe forms of energy that do not pose a threat to people or harm the planet. In doing so, they are returning to many early types of renewable energy that were used centuries ago. But they are using new, more-evolved forms of engineering to harness the power. This evolution in energy engineering is solving many of the issues we face around our need for energy and is paving the way for a brighter, more sustainable future.

People are also concerned that another disaster such as Chenobyl (shown here) could occur again.

CHAPTER 2

A SUNNY EVOLUTION

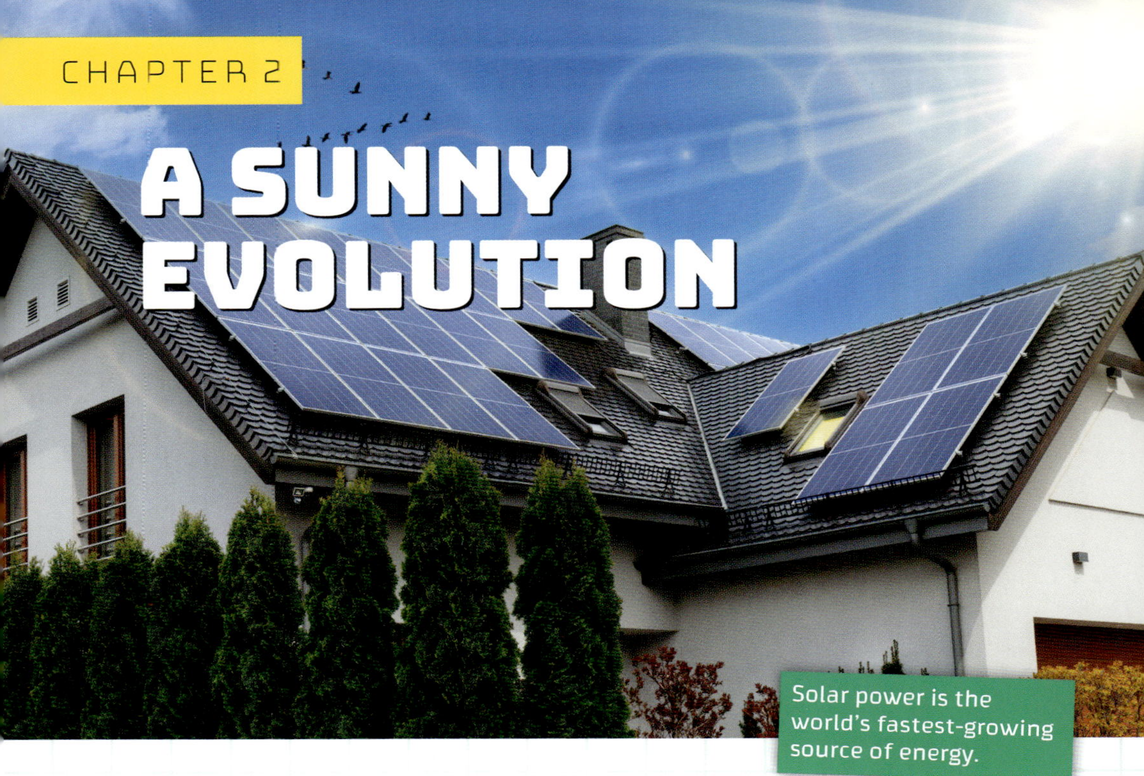

Solar power is the world's fastest-growing source of energy.

The sun is a star: a huge ball of incredibly hot gas that is powered by nuclear reactions at its core. This star produces enormous amounts of energy. Solar power is the way in which scientists have found ways to use some of that energy to meet our growing need for power.

Endless Energy

Our brilliant, powerful sun is a staggering 93 million miles (150 million km) away from Earth. However, every hour enough energy from this glowing ball reaches the planet to meet the world's entire energy needs for a year! And it takes that energy just 8 minutes to get to Earth. The sun provides energy in the form of light and heat. Capturing the energy from the sun is not without its challenges, but engineers have found smart ways to overcome those problems and capture some of the enormous energy created by our star.

Capturing the Heat

Using the heat of the sun is called thermal power or concentrated solar power (CSP). In countries that have warm and sunny climates, the sun's heat is used to heat water. A solar water heater called a collector is installed on the roof of a building and used to catch the sunlight. Flat plate collectors are most often used. They have a glass cover beneath which is a network of tubes filled with liquid. The liquid heats up in the sun and in turn heats a container of water. That heated water is then pumped into a storage tank either inside or outside the building.

Cooking with the Sun

Engineers have also found ways of using the sun for cooking. Millions of people around the world do not have electricity. They cook over fires that are fueled by wood or animal waste. The smoke from these fuels is very bad for human health. It also pollutes the atmosphere. Energy engineering innovators have come up with a smart plan to fix this problem: solar ovens.

HOW IT WORKS:
A SOLAR OVEN

A solar oven is a box surrounded by reflective panels made from material such as aluminum. The panels direct sunlight onto food, which is placed inside a closed cooking pot inside the box. The cooking pot is usually dark in color or lined with dark materials. That helps the pot absorb more sunlight because dark colors absorb heat more easily than light colors. The food is cut into small pieces before cooking, to make it easier to heat through. The oven is then put out in the sunshine, and the food is cooked.

Cooking with solar power is particularly helpful in places that are remote.

Solar, Big and Small

Solar heat is used on a large scale as well as on a small scale. In recent decades, huge thermal power plants have been built to generate electricity. There are two main types of thermal power plants. The first collects the sun's energy using rows of long, rectangular curved mirrors. The mirrors focus sunlight onto tubes that run down their length and heat up the fluid inside them. That hot fluid is then sent to a central location. There it is used to boil water, which creates steam that drives a generator to produce electricity. The mirrors move with the sun, to keep light focused on the tubes during the day.

A newer design uses flat mirrors, called heliostats, which reflect sunlight onto a tower at the center of a field. Concentrated sunlight inside the tower heats water to produce steam for the generator. Heliostats amplify, or increase, the sun's power up to 1,500 times more efficiently than older systems.

This concentrating solar power tower plant is near Seville, in Spain.

BIG Breakthroughs

The world's population is constantly growing. In large developing countries, such as India, more and more people are becoming able to afford the things that use electricity. That includes heating and cooling systems. It also includes the machines that many take for granted as part of modern life, such as computers, televisions, washing machines, refrigerators, and more. The rural areas of developing countries, however, often do not have a reliable electricity grid that can deliver power to every home. A solution to this problem is solar power.

Solar power can provide energy on both a small and large scale. On a small scale, a solar power installation on a single building can provide it with off-grid power at any time the sun shines. This engineering solution is a win-win in developing countries that get a lot of sunshine, such as much of India. Solar power installations could dramatically improve life for many people in rural parts of the world that do not have access to on-grid energy.

In the same way that solar power can be used to heat things up, it can also be used to cool them down. For many countries in which people live off-grid without electricity to power a refrigerator, keeping food cool and fresh can be a problem. A solar-powered refrigerator provides an easy solution to the issue for both ordinary people and farmers who need to store their fruit and vegetable crops before they sell them.

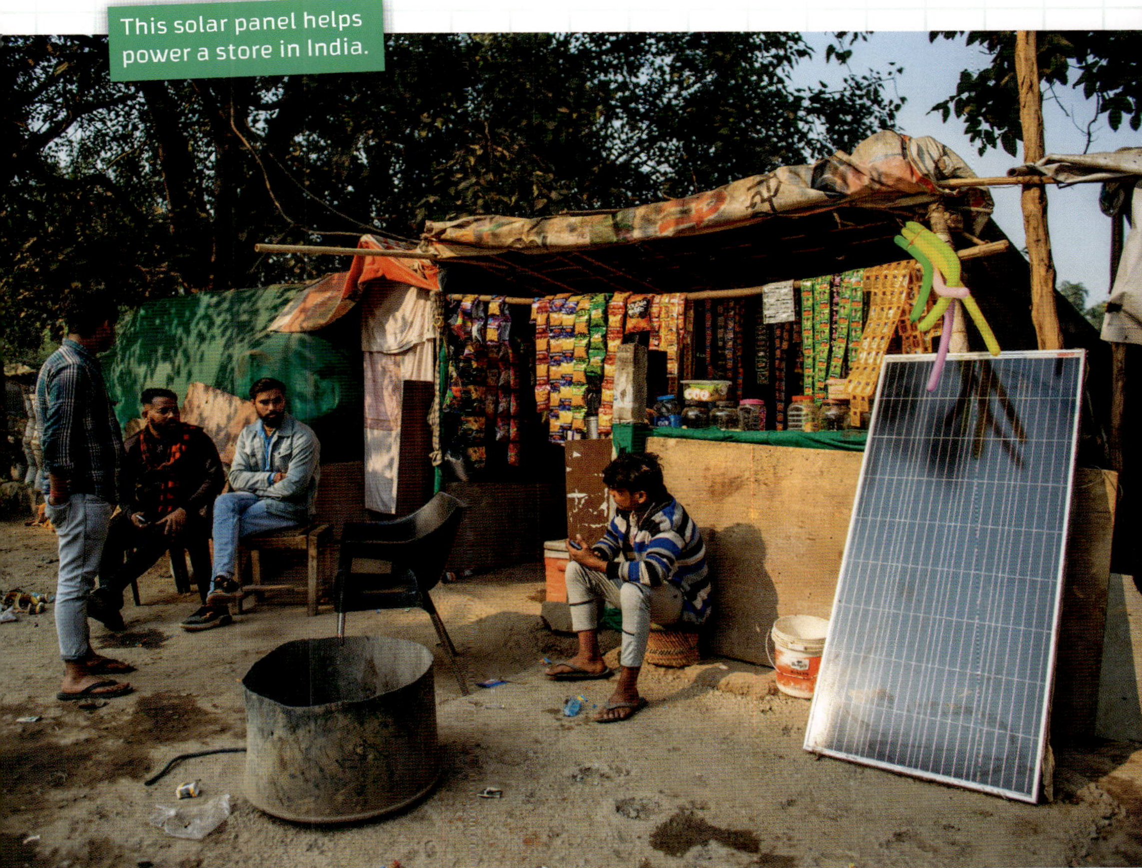

This solar panel helps power a store in India.

The Power of a Panel

The engineering innovation that uses sunlight for energy is the solar panel. Electricity is made from sunlight in a process called photovoltaics, or PV. During the last two decades, engineers have improved solar panel technology to a point where it can be used on a big scale. Today, the technology is efficient, flexible, and relatively cheap. It is providing people in many places with a viable alternative to fossil fuel.

The Story of the Solar Panel

In 1954, scientists discovered that a substance called silicon creates an electric charge when placed in sunlight. This was a breakthrough moment. Soon after, chips made from silicon were used to power small devices such as calculators and watches. Today, silicon is used in solar panels to create energy.

HOW IT WORKS: A SOLAR PANEL

Solar panels are made up of many small units called solar cells. Each cell has several layers that work together to make electricity. The top layer is glass, which lets sunlight pass through. Below is a coating that stops sunlight from bouncing off, helping the cell absorb more energy. Underneath, there are thin layers of a material called silicon. Silicon is specially treated with chemicals to create tiny particles, called electrons, that can move easily. When sunlight hits the silicon, the energy from the sun excites the electrons, which makes them move. This movement creates an electric current, which flows along wires connected to the panel.

Solar panels are being assembled by robots at this factory.

Solar panels must consistently face the sun to gather as much energy as possible.

Installing Solar Panels

PV cells are joined together to make panels. They are then installed on the roof of a building. The number of panels used depends on how much power is going to be needed in the building. The panels must be installed so they get as much sunlight as possible. In places in the northern hemisphere, this usually means putting them on a south-facing roof, tilted upward. A lot of heat is not good for solar panels because it makes them perform poorly. A panel will produce more electricity on a sunny, cold day than on a sunny, hot day.

ENGINEERING SOLUTIONS

Some buildings cannot be used for rooftop solar panels because they do not face the sun efficiently. Engineers have developed a smart solution to this problem: a solar-tracking mount. This innovative device securely holds PV panels and gradually rotates throughout the day to follow the sun's position in the sky. That allows the panels to capture as much sunlight as possible for optimal energy generation. The mounts can also be installed on the ground, making them even more flexible and useful.

Changing Electricity

Solar panels positioned on rooftops are connected to a battery, which stores the electricity they produce. Electricity can flow as either direct current (DC) or alternating current (AC). Solar panels generate DC electricity, but buildings use AC electricity because it is more practical for powering appliances and transmitting over long distances. To solve this, a solar power system uses an inverter to convert DC into AC. The inverter is kept inside the building, and from there, the electricity is directed to a fuse box. This distributes it through wires to supply power and lighting throughout the building.

ENGINEERING SOLUTIONS

PV panels generate electricity only when sunlight shines on them. When the sun shines directly, they can produce large amounts of electricity. But what happens when the sun is low in the sky or it's cloudy? Engineers have solved this problem by developing systems to store the solar energy in batteries. These batteries save electricity produced during sunny periods, making it available when the sun doesn't shine. Batteries also act as a backup energy source during power outages, ensuring people can still access electricity even when the grid is down.

Solar panels on the roof of a building capture energy which is then converted in an inverter.

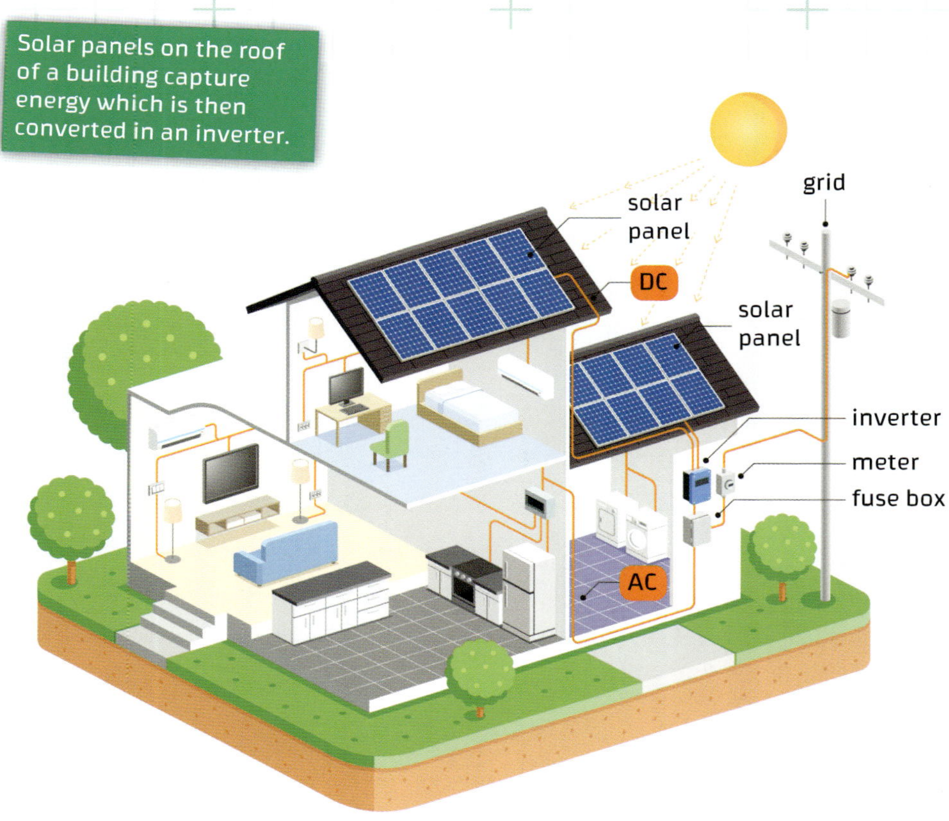

Large solar plants, like this one in India, are designed to capture the maximum amount of energy.

Energy for Everyone

Many individuals are installing solar panels on their homes or office buildings today. By doing so they can generate their own electricity from a renewable source. However, not everyone can install solar panels on their buildings, so how can energy from solar power be provided to everyone? The answer is a solar power plant. Solar power plants are large areas where solar panels have been erected to capture energy from the sun. These areas of land often have hundreds or even thousands of PV panels. They spread out across the land, tilting upward toward the sun. The panels are all connected to a central hub where the electricity is collected before it is distributed.

Following the Sun

To make sure the panels collect as much sunlight as possible they are often mounted on trackers rather than being fixed in position. That allows them to follow the movement of the sun as it passes across the sky. Using mounted trackers is a smart idea—it can increase the amount of electricity a solar plant produces by up to 20 percent.

Trackers make maximum use of available space. That means they can produce more energy without the need for more panels. They also move to match the sun's angle throughout the year. That helps them capture the maximum amount of energy during every season, including winter.

Solutions for Solar Space

In some countries where large areas of land for solar power plants are not readily available, engineers have another bright solution: floating solar power plants. In countries such as Japan many people live in a small area and space is hard to come by. However, Japan is made up of four islands and has a lot of lakes and reservoirs. By placing floating solar panels in these areas, solar power can be generated. These floating, space-saving solar power plants are called "floatovoltaics." An additional benefit of being on water is that it cools the panels, which improves their performance. The installation of the panels on the water also reduces the amount of water that evaporates from the lakes or reservoirs where they are placed.

Improving All the Time

Other innovations in engineering are taking place all the time in the energy industry, particularly in solar power because it is such a growing field. These developments are making it easier and cheaper to install solar power devices, which is contributing to the boom in the industry. One idea that engineers have come up with to get more power from PV panels is to make them double sided. New panels have cells fitted to both sides, so that they can capture solar power from each side. A double-sided panel does not produce twice the power because only one side gets the full force of sunlight. However, it can produce up to 25 percent more power, which is significant. Another smart idea is to paint the ground beneath the panels white, so that more light reflects off it and hits the panels.

These workers are cleaning and inspecting the panels on this floating solar plant.

Installing solar panels on apartment balconies is another smart engineering idea.

ENGINEERING SOLUTIONS

One particularly exciting innovation in solar power is the creation of solar roof tiles. They look just like ordinary roof tiles, but include invisible solar cells. These tiles can capture the energy of the sun, which is then converted into electricity and used to power the building. Many people prefer the look of the tiles to solar panels, and that could make more people more likely to use them on their buildings.

New Storage Systems

Engineers have also come up with better solutions for solar power storage. New and improved batteries are being developed all the time. Developers are also building battery storage into solar power plants. Excess energy that is created by the plants can be stored and then released when it is needed.

One of the most exciting current developments in solar power storage is advanced batteries, including lithium-ion and flow batteries, which can store a lot of energy. These systems allow homes, schools, and businesses to rely more on solar power, even at night or during cloudy weather.

Hardworking Windows

The growth in engineering in the energy industry looks set to continue, with new inventions appearing year on year. One of the most exciting is solar-powered windows. Engineers believe that if every building could use its windows to create electricity, that would transform the way we heat and power our homes, offices, and other buildings. In effect, every building would be a mini power plant!

The science behind this supersmart idea is complex. Instead of silicon, another material would be used within the solar cells: tiny particles called quantum dots. They conduct electricity and are included in the transparent material that is put over the window glass. When sunlight hits them, they concentrate its energy. Research is underway to develop the cells and also to make double-pane windows that can create shade as well as electricity.

The Solar Dome Planetarium and Auditorium in Kolkata, India, has solar panels on its outer walls to harness clean, sustainable energy.

BIG Breakthroughs

Scientists are exploring ways to capture more energy from the sun. The visible spectrum, which includes the light we see, is only a small part of the electromagnetic waves that make up sunlight. Beyond the visible range are ultraviolet (UV) and infrared waves. Infrared waves are already used in technologies like remote controls for televisions. Energy engineers are now developing solar panels that can capture infrared waves, enabling us to harness even more energy from the sun.

Transforming the Future

Another groundbreaking idea engineers are working on involves combining photovoltaics and solar thermal power into a single system. When a photovoltaic (PV) panel generates electricity, it also produces heat. Until now, much of this heat has been wasted, just flowing into the surrounding air. However, an amazing technology known as solar thermophotovoltaics (STPV) captures this heat energy and then uses it to make the panel's ability to generate electricity even better.

This process involves adding a special new layer to the solar cell's structure. This layer absorbs the excess heat and converts it into light of a specific wavelength. That light is then reflected onto another solar cell, where it is used to generate additional electricity in the usual way. By recycling the heat energy that was previously lost, STPV hugely increases the efficiency of solar panels.

Engineers estimate that combining photovoltaic and solar thermal power could capture up to 80 percent of the sunlight's energy! That is a huge improvement over the solar panels we currently use, which only collect about 30 percent of sunlight energy. If solar thermophotovoltaics technology becomes available around the world, it could completely change the solar power industry. It could help end the use of fossil fuels, cut harmful emissions, and offer clean energy solutions for homes, schools, and businesses everywhere.

Solar Thermophotovoltaics (STPV) researchers at UC Davis College of Engineering in California are searching for new solutions to help us capture even more solar power.

CHAPTER 3

A WINDY EVOLUTION

We have already learned that there is nothing new about using the wind for energy. People have been doing so for centuries. However, modern use of wind for energy really took off in the 1980s when engineers created enormous turbines to harness the power of the wind. Since then, using wind power for energy grew rapidly and today it is a huge industry. In the United States alone, wind power has grown significantly. In 1990 it provided less than 1 percent of all energy used by the country but today, it provides about 10 percent of the country's total energy. Like solar power, wind power is a renewable energy and engineers are working on ever-more inventive ways to use this natural energy to power our future.

Farming the Wind

Although it is huge, just one wind turbine does not generate a lot of energy. That is why wind turbines are usually grouped together. Many turbines cover large areas of land and these groupings of turbines are called wind farms. Wind farms are established in places that receive a lot of wind, such as the tops of smooth hills, open plains, coastlines, and open water.

Like solar power, wind power is not reliable all day, all year around. Some days are windier than others and certain times of the year have more wind than others. Energy companies have to gather a lot of information about the geography and weather patterns of places before they decide to erect wind farms there.

The length of the blades is the biggest factor in determining the amount of electricity a wind turbine can generate. For that reason, they are generally made as long as possible. Turbines can be as tall as 20-story buildings and have blades that stretch more than 100 feet (30 m) long.

A mechanical system inside a wind turbine converts wind energy into electricity.

HOW IT WORKS:
A WIND TURBINE

A wind turbine typically has three blades that rotate like airplane propellers. As wind flows over the blades, it creates lift, causing them to spin. The spinning blades are connected to a generator inside the turbine's nacelle. This generator converts the energy into electricity. The electricity is then sent down to ground level, where it is either stored in batteries or sent to the electrical grid.

ENGINEERING SOLUTIONS

Storms can be extremely destructive, but engineers believe they could be useful to us because of the energy they contain. Huge amounts of energy are created by storms called typhoons. Engineers are looking at creating turbines that can capture this enormous energy. A prototype for these turbines has many vertical blades joined at the top and bottom, which spin as the storm passes over them, to harness its energy.

Engineering Out at Sea

The wind usually blows more strongly and more regularly out at sea than it does on land. That is why wind farms are often positioned at sea. They are called offshore wind farms. One of the challenges engineers have had to overcome when designing wind turbines to be positioned out at sea is the conditions there. Salty sea air eats away at some metals and storm-force winds can blow at sea. Strong waves pound away at wind turbines when weather conditions are fierce, too. Turbines need to be made from material that can withstand erosion and stand firm even in extreme wind and lashing waves.

ENGINEERING SOLUTIONS

Another challenge with offshore wind farms is transporting the energy they generate back to shore. This problem is overcome with another engineering solution: huge power cables. The cables are buried under the ocean floor and carry energy from the turbines back to land. Installing the cables is expensive and difficult because cables can be easily damaged at sea. Electricity can "leak" from the cables before reaching land.

Engineers are constantly working on creating improved cables that are less likely to be damaged and leak energy. One of the latest innovations includes cables and cable systems with inbuilt sensors. They monitor the condition of the cables and report on any issues. That might include the amount of electricity leaking and wear and tear of the cable fabric. Engineers back on land monitor the faults and quickly repair them before too much damage is caused.

Cables carry the energy created by offshore wind farms to the land.

This offshore wind farm is positioned off the coast of the Netherlands.

Storing the Energy

One of the other problems with wind power is that it cannot be relied upon every day to provide people with the energy that they need. When the wind blows, turbines can generate a good amount of energy. But on a calm day, that energy drops. If there is a high demand for energy that day, that will be a problem. Engineers are working on ways to store energy created by wind turbines so that when the wind does not blow, there is still a good supply of energy for people to use.

One solution to storing wind energy is to use hydroelectric dams. Excess electricity from wind farms can be used to pump water to a reservoir at a dam nearby. When more electricity is needed, the water is released from the dam and its movement is used to drive huge turbines that generate electricity.

Engineers are also working on ways to build huge banks of batteries to store excess wind energy. They are exploring turning the energy into fuel in the form of hydrogen. Hydrogen is one of the elements in water and can be released from water in a process that uses electricity.

Sharing the Energy

Grids that distribute the electricity can also be made bigger—by connecting grids of several countries or states. By doing so, energy could be shared over a wider area. If the wind is not blowing in one area, it may well be blowing somewhere else. The energy created there could then be used in places where it is not currently windy. This system of sharing energy across large areas could be one smart solution to our future energy issues.

Wind turbine blades can be 200 feet (61 m) above ground and 100 feet (30 m) long. Drones can easily reach these heights and fly along the full length of the blades to inspect them.

Maintaining Turbines

Wind turbines are complex machines, and complicated engineering is involved in keeping them working. Turbines are constantly battered by weather, both on land and offshore. They must be constantly monitored to ensure they are working and repairs must be made as soon as they are needed. That constant monitoring and maintenance requires some smart engineering solutions.

Drone Inspectors

Wind turbines stand tall either on land or out at sea. They are not quick or easy for a person to scale. But, for a drone, inspecting a turbine is easy. Drones are often used to check turbines for damage. They inspect the turbines and take photographs of them. That information is then used by engineers on the ground, who assess any problems. A drone can make a full inspection of a turbine in just 8 minutes.

The turbine blades also contain inbuilt sensors. They sense things like vibrations, temperature, and structural strain, which helps in predicting potential failures. The sensors constantly feed information to machine operators on the ground. The operators use software that can quickly assess data from the sensors to build a picture of where and when problems are likely to occur. With that knowledge, operators can predict what repairs are likely and plan for them.

ENGINEERING SOLUTIONS

Inspecting wind turbines on land is much easier than inspecting those out at sea. While drones can quickly check the tops of offshore turbines, inspecting parts below the waterline is much harder. Engineers have developed innovative solutions, like underwater robots, to address this challenge. These machines can capture detailed images of submerged turbine components, making it easier to detect problems such as corrosion or cracks. In the future, robots might even repair turbines underwater, saving time and ensuring turbines stay efficient.

An Artificial Future

In the future, artificial intelligence (AI) may further revolutionize the wind power industry. Drones are already used in turbine inspection, and turbines are fitted with sensors that detect problems and collect huge amounts of data about weather and other factors. When that data is collected, smart computer software will be able to analyze it. AI will then be able to predict when the wind will blow stronger or when repairs may be necessary. We may even see robots crawling up turbines in the future, checking for damage and carrying out repairs. A crawling robot could travel up and down the surface of a blade with ease and carry out repairs as it goes.

Repairing a damaged rotor blade on a wind turbine is much easier and safer for a robot than it is for a person.

Shaped for Efficiency

Wind turbine design is changing rapidly in the quest to capture more energy from the wind. Today's turbines have taller towers and longer blades. Engineers are also working on ways to make smaller turbines more effective. Wind turbines that are only 30 feet (9 m) tall have been fitted with vertical blades that turn like a spinning top. The turbines are grouped together in a diamond pattern, similar to that used by schools of fish as they swim together. The pattern helps the blades capture more energy.

In Deep Water

Engineering improvements in ways to carry electricity to the grid are also underway. Engineers are looking at installing cables as far as 1.8 miles (3 km) below the ocean, so that electricity can be carried from deep-ocean wind farms in the future.

Engineers are also exploring ways of erecting wind farms even farther out at sea, where the wind blows more strongly. In the United States, about 90 percent of available wind energy is in waters that are too deep for the turbine technology that is currently available. Conditions in deep water are also extremely harsh, with fast-blowing winds and extremely powerful waves. Turbines that can survive these conditions must be carefully engineered.

Small vertical wind turbines take up little space and can be positioned wherever wind power can be captured. These turbines are on the top of a building in the Netherlands.

Spinning Flowers

Flower Turbines is a company that is helping to transform energy supply in cities like New York. Each turbine has a flower-like shape that captures wind from any direction, making them efficient even in low-wind areas. Flower Turbines have a special "bouquet effect"—when the turbines are placed together it greatly boosts their energy output.

A First for Deep Sea

In 2017, the world's first-ever floating wind farm was opened. It was designed to deal specifically with the problems of positioning wind turbines in harsh and extreme environments, such as out at sea. The Hywind floating wind farm is positioned 15.5 miles (25 km) off the coast of Scotland in the United Kingdom (UK). The turbines are suitable for water up to 2,625 feet (800 m) deep. The successful installation of the wind farm has paved the way for similar installations in other waters around the world.

A First for Energy Storage

Hywind engineers have also created a powerful battery storage solution for the wind farm. Named Batwind, it uses a large collection of batteries that can hold as much electricity as more than 128,000 smartphones. The storage system has made it possible to store energy produced from an offshore wind farm for the first time.

HOW IT WORKS: BATWIND

Batwind is positioned on the coast where the Hywind cables come ashore. The system automatically understands when to store power and when to send it to the grid. It does that based on information such as the weather, time of day, and the amount of power already in the grid.

This diagram shows how electricity is transported along undersea cables from turbines out at sea to the Batwind storage area.

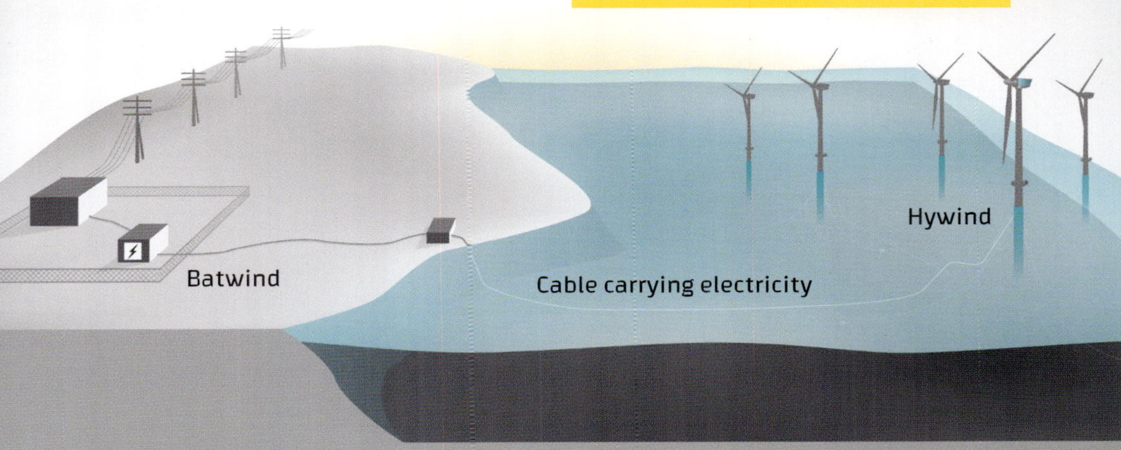

Power in the Sky

Most wind turbines are about 329 feet (100 m) from the ground. There, the wind speed is about 11 miles per hour (18 kph). But at a height of 3,282 feet (1,000 m) above the ground, the average wind speed nearly doubles to 20 miles per hour (32 kph). At that height, the wind speed is also more consistent than at lower levels. When the wind speed nearly doubles, it provides eight times more energy. For that reason, engineers are exploring the idea of airborne wind turbines.

Floating Turbines

Technicians at the Massachusetts Institute of Technology (MIT) have created a turbine that is held inside a giant helium-filled ring-shaped balloon. It floats 1,000 feet (305 m) in the air and captures wind currents that are five to eight times more powerful than breezes at ground level. The turbine generates enough energy to power more than 12 households. This could be extremely useful in remote areas that do not have access to the grid. There, the turbine could provide energy for small communities.

The Buoyant Airborne Turbine (BAT) is designed to float up to 2,000 feet (609 m) in the air, capturing stronger and more consistent winds.

Soaring Turbines

Another option that engineers are exploring is kite turbines. They are fixed to the ground by a long wire, but swoop into the sky, flying in loops. As they fly, the rotors on the wings of the turbines spin in the wind. That generates electricity that is sent down the wire to the ground. In testing, a kite turbine soared up to 984 feet (300 m) above the ground, where it captured the energy from fast-blowing winds.

Kiwee One is a portable wind turbine designed to harness renewable energy anywhere.

ENGINEERING SOLUTIONS

Imagine if we could also capture the whooshing air created as cars and other vehicles drive at speed along roads and highways. Traffic is a problem because it creates pollution, but what if we could turn that problem into a form of renewable energy? Engineers are working on turbines that capture the fast-moving air created by moving vehicles. The turbine is shaped like a twisted helix, with turbines. When placed along a highway, airport runway, or subway track, the turbines change the moving air into energy. At the same time, the turbines filter pollutants created by the traffic from the air, cleaning it while providing renewable energy.

The turbines could also solve some of our modern-day energy problems in another way—by providing energy to people who live off-grid in rural communities. Because the turbines are portable, they can be taken wherever needed. That means people could easily fix them to the roofs of their buildings or place them in areas that are windy and collect the energy that the turbines generate. This would be a smart solution for people who live in developing countries without access to electricity, as well as people in more developed countries who live off-grid.

Fast-moving traffic could be used to help us harness energy.

CHAPTER 4

A WATERY EVOLUTION

Some of the most famous examples of hydroelectric power include the Three Gorges Dam in China and the Hoover Dam in the United States (shown above).

Just as people have used solar and wind power since early times, so too have they used the power from water. Over the centuries, engineers have developed ingenious ways to harness this renewable source of energy. Today, the power from water is captured using smart forms of engineering, including hydroelectric power, pumped storage hydropower, tidal power, wave power, and marine current power.

What Is Hydroelectric Power?

Hydroelectric power is the use of flowing water to generate electricity. This power is usually created in two ways: the first with the use of conventional dams and the second with run-of-the-river systems.

Many countries have built large-scale hydroelectric power plants that use dams to store river water in a reservoir. Water is released from the reservoir and then flows through turbines. As the turbines turn, they generate energy. Dams have been used for hundreds of years as a way to contain and control water, but a more recent and less environmentally harmful form of harnessing the power of water are run-of-the-river systems. These systems divert a section of river flow through a canal or a penstock and the flow then spins a turbine. The system does not depend on the building of reservoirs, and so has a smaller environmental footprint.

Giant Batteries

Pumped storage hydropower is a means of using water power that has been stored as needed. During periods of low electricity demand, excess electrical power is used to pump water from a lower reservoir to an upper reservoir. Then, during periods of high electrical demand, the stored water is released back to the lower reservoir through turbines. As the turbines spin, they generate electricity. Bath County Pumped Storage Station in Virginia is a good example of such a system.

BIG Breakthroughs

Like wind power, engineers are working on ways to make hydro power available on a small scale as well as a large scale. For people in rural and developing communities who do not have access to electricity, hydro power could be a solution to their energy needs if they live near a river. Small-scale run-of-the-river systems are often used by communities in remote or rural areas to provide them with energy. Eco-friendly resorts and activity centers near rivers are also using these micro water power solutions to provide them with clean energy.

Bath County Pumped Storage Station in Virginia is the largest pumped storage station in the world.

Moving water contains powerful energy.

Using the Power of the Tides

Tidal stream generators capture the kinetic energy of moving water in a similar way to underwater wind turbines. They are especially useful in places that have strong tidal currents. Tidal streams are strong and predictable water currents that are created by the rise and fall of tides. Tides are currents that occur as the gravitational forces of the moon and sun act on ocean waters, causing them to rise and fall. As moving water passes through the tidal stream generators, they convert the kinetic energy of the water into electrical energy.

A Power We Can Rely On

Using tidal power is a significant achievement for energy engineers. Tidal power is very predictable—the tides rise and fall every day, without fail. Unlike solar and wind power, we know exactly how much power we can get from tidal energy each day. That makes it a dependable source of power. Water also has a higher energy density than air. That means when measured, the same amounts of water and air have different amounts of energy—water contains far more energy than the same amount of air. For that reason, we can generate more electrical energy from smaller amounts of water than we can from wind. Another advantage is that tidal generators are underwater—because they are not easily seen they do not have a visual impact on the environment. Many people prefer them to wind turbines for that reason.

Not Without Challenges

However, the challenge to engineers is to create tidal stream generators that do not greatly impact the environment. There are concerns about the effect that the generators could have on marine life. Building and maintaining the generators is also costly and difficult compared to land turbines. Finding solutions to these critical issues will be one of the future goals for innovative energy engineers.

HOW IT WORKS:

A TIDAL STREAM GENERATOR

A tidal stream generator is made up of a rotor, nacelle, generator, the supporting structure, and electrical cables. These parts work together in the following way:

Rotor: This part is made up of blades that are moved by tidal currents. The blades are designed to capture the energy from the flow of water. They may have horizontal blades, like wind turbines, or vertical blades.

Nacelle: This contains the generator and other mechanical parts of the generator. The rotor is connected to the generator by a shaft inside the nacelle.

Generator: As the rotor blades turn, they spin the shaft connected to the generator. That converts the mechanical energy from the rotating shaft into electrical energy.

Supporting structure: The turbine is held to the seabed using a fixed foundation or mooring system, a little like an anchor. This keeps it steady in the tidal stream.

Electrical cables: Electricity is transmitted to the shore through underwater cables. At the shore, the energy is transferred to the grid.

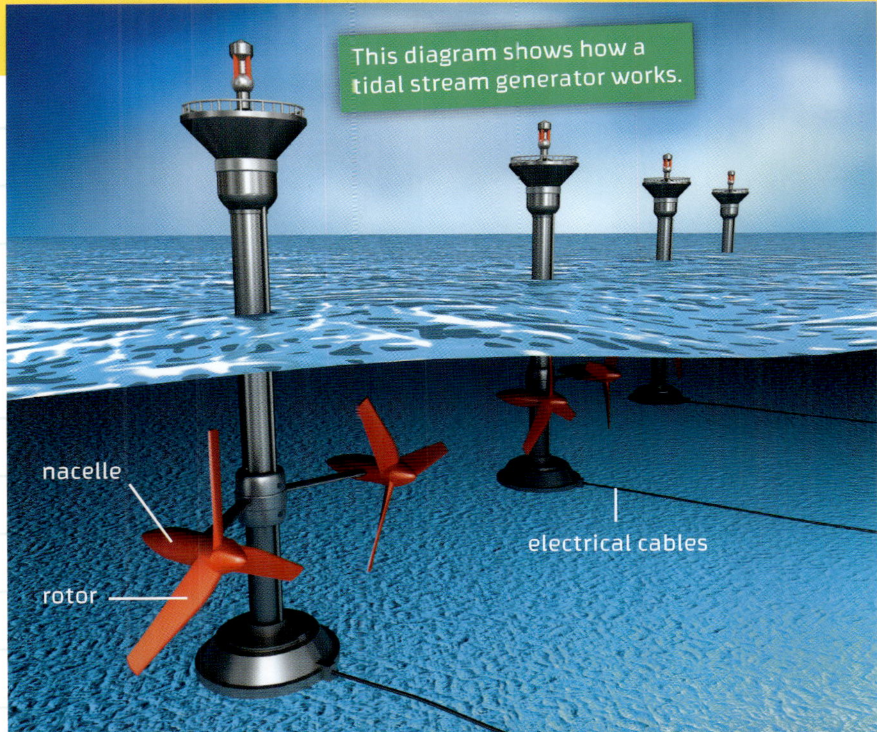

This diagram shows how a tidal stream generator works.

Wave energy is extremely powerful.

The Power of Waves

Every day, waves rise and fall at sea and crash against coastlines. The energy they produce as they do so is impressive to see. But what if we could capture that energy and use it to power our lives? Engineers have come up with ways to do just that.

Up and Down

Oscillating water columns (OWCs) are structures that use the rise and fall of sea waves to compress air in a chamber. That compressed air drives turbines, which generate electricity. Each OWC has a partly submerged chamber with an opening below the waterline. As waves pass, the water enters and leaves the chamber. That makes the OWC move up and down. This is called oscillation, and it affects air that is trapped in the upper part of the chamber.

ENGINEERING SOLUTIONS

Wave power provides many solutions to our current energy problems. The energy of the oceans' waves is constant and will never run out. That means we can depend on it as a source of power forever, unlike fossil fuels. Waves are also predictable because their patterns can be forecasted reasonably accurately. That means we have a good idea of how much energy we can get from waves, and when. OWCs lie beneath the ocean surface, which means they do not have a visual impact on the environment. That is another factor that makes wave power attractive.

The oscillation of the water column compresses (squashes) and decompresses (opens up) the trapped air as it presses on it while rising, then reduces the pressure as it subsides. That causes the air to move in and out of the chamber—and as it does so, it moves through a turbine. The turbine blades rotate as air moves over them, to generate energy. That energy drives a generator, which produces electricity.

New Ideas in the Pipeline

Engineers are always searching for new ways to use the power of water as a renewable energy source while protecting the environment. They aim to create designs that work efficiently and do not harm nature. These discoveries may lead to better, cleaner energy for the future. Some of the ideas in development include:

Fish-friendly turbines: These turbines are designed to allow fish to pass through them more safely. Their fish-friendly design reduces the number of fish that are harmed by water-based turbines.

Variable-speed turbines: These devices alter the speed at which they turn to match the river flow—when the river flows quickly, they flow quickly, and when the river flows slowly, they do the same. That allows them to capture the maximum amount of energy.

Using water treatment plants: Using the excess pressure in water treatment facilities to generate electricity is a smart way to produce energy in urban areas.

Stormwater energy capture: Using the energy from stormwater runoff in urban areas is another way to turn excess water into renewable energy.

This OWC is located in Honolulu, Hawaii.

CHAPTER 5

A GEOTHERMAL EVOLUTION

The heat below Earth's surface is called geothermal energy. We cannot feel this energy when we stand on the ground, but it lies beneath our feet—and there is a lot of it. The Romans used the heat of Earth by constructing their public baths around hot springs. Thousands of years later, energy engineering has evolved to make even more inventive use of our planet's underground heat.

Why Is Earth Hot?

Our planet is made up of four major layers. On the outside is the crust. This is the solid rock we live on. It is 15 to 35 miles (24 to 56 km) thick under land. Under the oceans, it is thinner—about 3 to 5 miles (5 to 8 km) thick. Below the crust is the mantle. This is a much thicker layer of solid and molten, or melted, rock. It is about 1,800 miles (2,900 km) thick. Below that is the outer core, which is 1,500 miles (2,414 km) of incredibly hot magma. At the center of Earth is the inner core. It is about 1,500 miles (2,414 km) across and made of solid iron. The temperature there is about 10,800 degrees Fahrenheit (5,982 °C). That is as hot as the surface of the sun. The temperature of the rock decreases toward the outer layers. Where the mantle meets the crust, it is about 393 degrees Fahrenheit (200 °C).

The crust is not solid. It is broken into pieces called tectonic plates. In the places where the plates meet, the magma beneath Earth's crust rises closer to the surface. The rocks and underground water in these places absorb the heat from the magma. That is the heat that we use for geothermal energy.

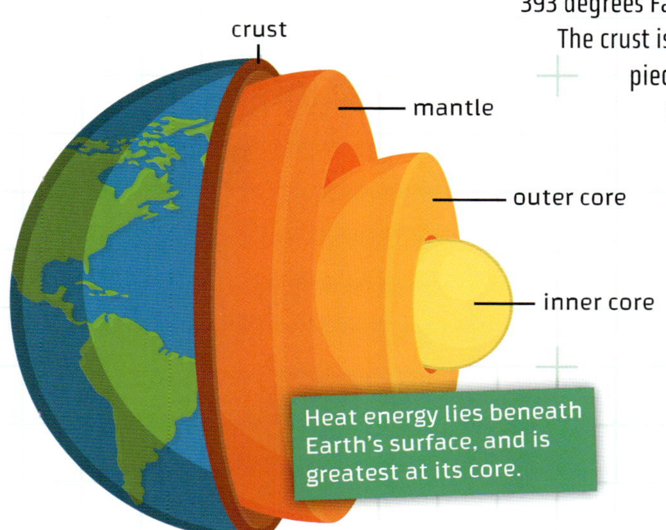

Heat energy lies beneath Earth's surface, and is greatest at its core.

This geyser is in Iceland, Europe. It is a country with a lot of geothermal energy.

HOW IT WORKS:

USING GEOTHERMAL ENERGY

The Romans used geothermal energy by building baths around places where hot water naturally bubbled to the surface. Today, engineers have created more sophisticated systems to harness the power beneath Earth's surface. They use three methods:

Direct use: Heated water from under the ground rises to the surface as hot springs or geysers. It can be used for purposes such as heating buildings or filling swimming pools.

Geothermal heat pumps: Underground heat is used to warm or cool water as it flows through pipes laid beneath the surface. The heated or cooled water is then sent to buildings for temperature regulation.

Electricity generation: Underground heat and water are used to produce electricity in geothermal power plants. The generated electricity is then fed into the power grid for widespread use.

Direct Use

Places that have a lot of hot water near the surface can use this water to heat buildings across large areas. The water can be piped directly to nearby offices, schools, and homes. Iceland is a country with a lot of geothermal energy. It has many underground hot water reservoirs and hot springs and geysers on its surface.

Geothermal Heat Pumps

In places where heat is not so readily available near the surface, its energy can still be used. This is done by sending water underground to be heated and then pumping it back to the surface. Engineers have created a system called a ground-source heat pump to do this. Today, some buildings, including homes, are fitted with this system.

The pump is connected to a series of pipes that are buried underground. A fluid, often water, is pumped through the pipes down below, where the water is heated by the ground. It is then pumped back up into the building, where it heats it. This is done by passing the water through a heat exchanger, which transfers the heat into the building's existing air handling and distribution system. If a superheater is used, it can heat the building's water too. After use, the water returns to the ground in a cooler form, where it is once again heated.

Geothermal power plants connect to the buildings that use their energy via a series of pipes.

In Iceland's capital city Reykjavik, a district heating system uses naturally heated water to provide heat for most of the buildings in the city.

Using Heat to Keep Cool

The same technology can also be used to keep buildings cool. If the temperature of the air is higher than the constant temperature below the ground, the water in the pipes will be hotter above ground. When it is pumped back into the ground, it loses some of that heat so that when it is pumped back up, it is cooler. That water can then be used to cool the building too.

Going Deeper to Heat Farther

Geothermal heat can also be used in another way. People drill even farther under the ground to create two wells. Water is pumped into one of them. It is heated by passing through rock underground, then pumped back up through the second well. Its energy is extracted and distributed to a number of buildings to supply heat. That is called district heating.

ENGINEERING SOLUTIONS

Geothermal energy has many advantages. It has little impact on the environment—geothermal power plants are far less polluting than power plants that burn fossil fuels. Unlike fossil fuels, they produce almost no harmful gases or air pollutants. Geothermal energy is also renewable, making it a sustainable option for future generations. It also provides consistent energy, regardless of weather conditions, unlike solar or wind power. These qualities make geothermal energy a great eco-friendly option.

Geothermal power plants use less land than other types of energy systems, so are a great choice when land is in short supply. They can also be built where land is used for farming or buildings, so they don't take up space that people need.

Electricity Generation

The third method we use to tap into geothermal energy is by using the steam from deep underground to make electricity. This takes place in a geothermal power plant. The electricity created is fed into the grid and then distributed where needed.

Generating electricity from geothermal power depends on water or steam at very high temperatures. The steam or water must be between 300 and 700 degrees Fahrenheit (149 and 371 °C). The power plant must be positioned closer to an underground reservoir of hot water or steam that is no more than 1 or 2 miles (1.6 or 3.2 km) beneath the surface. A deep well is drilled into the reservoir, the hot water is piped to the surface, then used to power a turbine that generates electricity.

Engineering in Industry

Industries in particular use a huge amount of heat in their processes, so this is an area where geothermal energy could provide great solutions. The energy source is especially useful for processes that need constant but relatively low heat, or for preheating liquids or materials before a high-heat process. The uses of geothermal energy in industry vary from drying timber and dyeing fabric to extracting gold and silver from rock. Drying is the most common industrial use of geothermal energy. That is because it needs a relatively low heat to be applied over a long period of time.

ENGINEERING SOLUTIONS

Geothermal power is also being used inventively in agriculture. Heating glasshouses with geothermal water maintains a constant temperature, which allows crops to grow more quickly and reliably. The water in the pipes can also be released inside the glasshouse, into the air. That increases humidity, or heat and water vapor, which is helpful for growing certain crops. The latest systems are finely tuned so they can be adapted to whatever crops are grown. For example, if crops need a good air flow and low humidity, the system is programmed to provide it. If crops need a lot of humidity and little air flow, the system is altered to match that need.

These glasshouses in Iceland are heated using geothermal power.

Power Plants That Use Earth's Heat

Geothermal energy power plants fall into three main categories. One uses dry steam, the second uses flash steam, and the third uses a binary cycle. All of them rely on very hot water in reservoirs up to 2 miles (3.2 km) below Earth's surface.

Dry Steam Power Plants

In a dry steam power plant, steam is piped directly from the ground up to the plant. There the steam is used to turn turbines that generate electricity. The first dry steam power plant was built in Italy more than 100 years ago, in a place where steam naturally spurted up from the ground. There was no need to dig a deep well to access it. Since then, power plants using deeply drilled wells have accessed the steam in many other places.

Flash Steam Power Plants

A flash steam power plant takes hot water under very high pressure from deep inside the well and changes it to steam at the surface. That is called flashing. The steam is then used to power turbines, which generate electricity. When the steam has cooled, it becomes water once more. It is then injected back into the ground, where it is used again. Most modern geothermal power plants are flash steam plants.

This dry steam power plant in California is one of a group of geothermal power plants in the Salton Sea and Imperial Valley area.

The Hellisheidi geothermal power plant in Iceland is a flash steam power plant.

Binary Cycle Power Plants

The third type of power plant design uses a system similar to the flash steam plant. However, instead of using the geothermal hot water to make steam, it transfers the heat into another liquid with a lower boiling point. The heat causes that liquid to turn into a gas, much like water turns to steam. This gas is then used to drive the turbines, which generate electricity. A key advantage of binary cycle power plants is their ability to operate using lower temperature geothermal resources, making them more versatile and accessible for areas with less intense geothermal heat. This design is called a binary cycle power plant.

ENGINEERING SOLUTIONS

The advantage of a binary cycle power plant is that it can use cooler water than a dry steam or flash steam power plant. The water it uses is around 225 to 360 degrees Fahrenheit (107 to 182 °C). Because the second liquid has a lower boiling point than water, the heating water does not need to be as hot. Underground reservoirs with a lower water temperature are more common than reservoirs with very hot water. For that reason, binary cycle power plants are more likely to be used in the industry in the future as geothermal energy becomes more widespread.

A Slinky Solution

Like all forms of energy sourcing, geothermal energy does not come without its challenges. One of them is that effective ground-source heat pumps require a wide network of underground pipes. That network can take up a lot of space, which may not always be available to some buildings. A smart engineering solution to this problem is a slinky-shaped coil of pipes. The design fits more pipes into a small area, which means that ground-source heat pumps can be more easily installed in buildings in areas that do not have a lot of space, such as cities.

Ingenious Equipment

Cutting into the ground to reach the heat that lies below also requires expensive equipment. Drilling through hard rock quickly wears out equipment such as a drill and the motor that powers it. Replacing that equipment over and over can be very expensive. One engineering solution to this problem is a drill made of extremely strong metal, fitted with a very powerful motor. The tough drill and supercharged motor can drill for many hours, reaching deep underground more quickly than traditional drills. Underground, high temperatures can also affect and damage equipment. The new system uses a very high-temperature lubricant in the drilling fluid to ensure the drill keeps working.

The coil of pipes for a heat pump system can be horizontal or vertical.

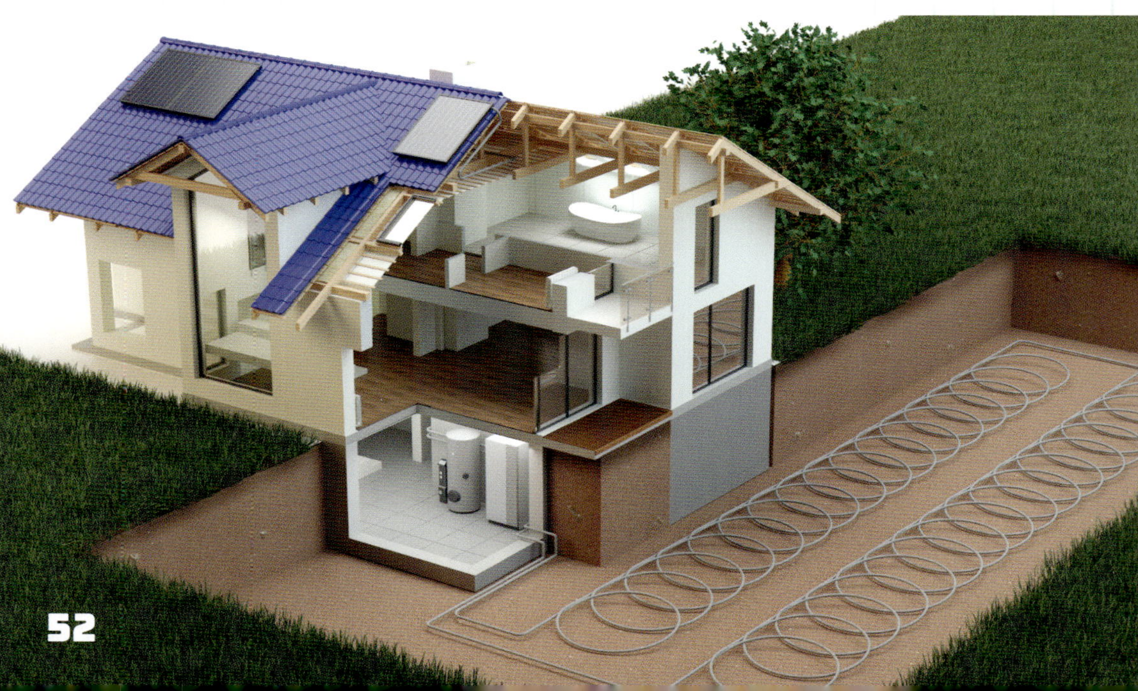

Drilling with Lasers

Engineers are also working on methods of drilling that use lasers. A laser is a very powerful bean of concentrated light. It can be used in drills to push through very hard rock. The laser hits the rock before the drill, and is contained within a jet of water. The laser energy starts to break up the rock and the water then continues that work by breaking off pieces of it. The drill then follows, but has a much clearer path to work through and is less likely to be damaged.

Engineers have installed a geothermal pipe to this new building to supply it with heated water.

BIG Breakthroughs

In the United States, an energy evolution in the geothermal industry is underway. It is called the Enhanced Geothermal System (EGS). It involves pumping water into naturally occurring cracks in the ground 2 to 3 miles (3.2 to 5 km) below the surface. The water opens up the cracks slightly, so that new reservoirs are made underground. In those reservoirs, the natural heat of Earth warms the water to around 600 degrees Fahrenheit (316 °C).

The hot water and the steam that is created are pumped back to a power plant at the surface. There, the steam turns turbines that produce electricity. The hot water is then cooled and returned underground, so the process can begin again. EGS can be used almost anywhere that suitable rock exists, so it has great potential for use in the energy industry.

THE FUTURE IS EVOLVING

People are inventive. We have found amazingly smart engineering solutions to our energy needs in the past and we will find similarly ingenious solutions in the future. There are already brilliant concepts in the pipeline for the energy industry, which looks set to be transformed in decades to come thanks to the work of our engineers.

Endless Energy

Nuclear fusion is one of the shining solutions for our energy future. It is what powers the stars in the universe, such as our sun. It is created at the sun's core, where it is incredibly hot. There, the high temperatures and the force of gravity cause atoms of hydrogen to squeeze together. As that happens, the hydrogen atoms turn into helium atoms. In that process, masses of heat and light energy are created. Just a small part of that heat lights and warms our planet, 93 million miles (150 million km) away! Imagine if we could create a fraction of that energy here on Earth. It would solve all our energy problems. Engineers are exploring just how we can do that.

A tokamak is a special machine that helps scientists copy the way that the sun creates power.

Engineers Working Together

Nuclear fusion is a very difficult process to recreate. It requires extremely high temperatures, so engineers are trying to find a way to create those temperatures and maintain them long enough for nuclear fusion to occur. Very high pressure is also needed to force hydrogen atoms to squeeze together. But we are getting closer to achieving the process and several exciting projects around the world are underway to do so. They include an international collaboration of 35 countries, including the United States. The project is called the International Thermonuclear Experimental Reactor (ITER).

Next Generation

Engineers are also working on next-generation solar cells. These are made of a material called perovskite. It has potential to be even more efficient than silicon in capturing solar power. It also makes the production of solar cells cheaper and much easier. The material allows for solar panels to be created in more flexible and lightweight forms, too. And of course, ever-evolving engineering is taking place in the wind, water, and geothermal industries. Over decades to come, we are likely to see even more inventive ways to use the power of our planet.

Perovskite solar cells could greatly improve our ability to use the energy of the sun.

EVOLVE AS AN ENGINEER

Smart engineering solutions to the world's problems require smart brains. Without the amazing engineering minds of the past, we'd never have created devices that make fire, harness the power of wind and water, or tap into the heat within Earth and the energy of the sun. Engineering is one of the most exciting fields to work in and one of the most rewarding. If you would like to build an engineering career, explore the following pages to discover how you could work in this ever-evolving field and help fix our energy issues.

EVOLVING CAREERS IN ENGINEERING

There are many exciting job opportunities within the energy industry for engineers. As this rapidly changing field develops, so too do the career options within it. Here are just some of the evolving engineering roles you could explore.

Renewable Energy Engineer

In this area, you would work on engineering solutions in the solar, wind, and geothermal energy fields. You could specialize to work as a solar energy engineer, wind energy engineer, or geothermal energy engineer. As a solar energy engineer you would focus on the design, installation, and improvement of solar power systems such as PV panels, solar thermal systems, and new technology such as perovskite solar cells. As a wind energy engineer, you would work on the design, construction, and maintenance of wind turbines, both offshore and onshore. As a geothermal energy engineer, you would specialize in finding new and more efficient ways to harness energy from within Earth.

Offshore energy engineers specialize in creating systems that harness energy from the ocean, including tidal, wave, and OTEC systems. You could also work as a subsea engineer to develop underwater infrastructure for offshore wind, wave, and tidal energy projects. You would likely design cables, foundation structures, and control systems.

Great engineering minds are finding smart solutions to our energy problems.

Engineers of today and the future will work with virtual reality (VR) to imagine green energy solutions.

Energy Storage Engineer

As a battery systems engineer your role would be to develop and improve energy storage systems, including battery systems. You could work as a hydrogen storage engineer and develop systems for storing hydrogen safely and efficiently so it could be used as a fuel.

Smart Grid Engineer

In this role, you would work on integrating renewable energy sources into the grid and making sure they work efficiently and reliably. You would likely work with technology such as AI. As an energy systems architect, your job would be to design and implement smart grid infrastructure. You would make sure the smart grid works properly and reaches all the consumers that need energy.

Carbon Capture Engineer

In this field, you would focus on creating technology that can capture carbon dioxide directly from the atmosphere. You could also work on processes to convert the captured carbon into useful products, such as fuels and building materials.

Fusion Energy Engineer

In this role, you would work on creating systems that can create nuclear fusion. You would design, build, and operate reactors designed to carry out that process.

Artificial Intelligence (AI) Engineer

An AI energy analyst uses AI to analyze energy use, and predict how to optimize it. They also use technology to figure out when and where maintenance will be needed in renewable energy systems.

How to Get into Engineering

If you think some or all of the roles outlined on the previous pages could be for you, the next steps in building a career in engineering start at school. Focus on STEM subjects because you will need qualifications in this area. STEM includes science, technology, engineering, and math. Engineers use math to problem solve and figure out designs, so it is an important skill to work on. Science is important too because you'll need to understand physical science concepts such as forces, energy, and materials.

STEM Clubs and Camps

Consider joining a STEM club. This is a great place to work on your engineering skills. Many schools have clubs that focus on robotics, coding, and engineering challenges. Taking part will give you important hands-on experience that will help set you up for a career in engineering. You could also try a STEM camp. Many summer camps are STEM-focused today, to help young people develop these important skills.

Consider Coding

Many areas of engineering require coding skills, so working on understanding the basics of coding is a great way to get into engineering. Try platforms such as Scratch, Python, or Blockly. Programming is very important in engineering fields such as robotics and electrical engineering. You can also work on simple projects such as games, apps, and easy robots to put what you have learned into practice.

STEM and robotics clubs and camps are great places to get some hands-on engineering experience.

Experimenting with robotics is a good way to learn important engineering skills.

Try Out Kits

Having fun with kits can be a great way to build your engineering skills while exploring exciting possibilities. Try working with LEGO™, Arduino, and similar kits to create robots, electronic devices, and gadgets. These kits allow you to experiment and learn how different components work together.

Any practical projects can fire up your engineering brain and show you how rewarding working in engineering can be. You can even customize your creations, solving problems to improve designs and make them more efficient. These hands-on activities spark creativity and show how engineering can make a big difference in everyday life.

Talk to Other Engineers

Tell your teachers that you are interested in engineering, and they may be able to put you in touch with engineers who could talk to you about career options. You may even be able to visit engineers at work and see what a day in the life in this career is like. School counselors are also great people to talk to about career options, and they may be able to find engineering mentors for you to talk to. They will also be able to advise on courses to take once you finish school that will help put you on your path to a bright future career in engineering.

Find Out More

When thinking about the next steps after school, spend time researching engineering programs at colleges and universities. The more you can find out now, the better placed you will be when the time comes to apply for a course.

GLOSSARY

absorb to take in or soak up

adapted made suitable for a new use or purpose

ancient Egyptians a powerful civilization that existed between 3100–30 BCE

ancient Greeks an advanced ancient civilization that lived in Greece around 2,500 years ago. The ancient Greeks developed a civilization that was rich in art, politics, engineering, and other forms of science

artificial intelligence (AI) software that performs tasks that normally require human intelligence

atmosphere the protective layers of gas that surround Earth

atom the basic unit of a chemical element

circulated moved continuously through a closed system or area

civilization a society that has a particular culture and way of life

clean energy energy that comes from renewable sources that cause zero emissions

climates general weather conditions of a given area

coal seam a layer of coal found within Earth's crust

collaboration working with one or more people to achieve a shared aim

compress to squeeze together

concentrate to gather together in a common location

conduct to transmit a form of energy, such as electricity

consumers people who buy and use goods and services

controversial describes something that causes disagreement

converting changing the form, character, or function of something

devices equipment that serves a special purpose

distributing dividing among several or many

drone a remote-controlled aircraft or flying device that has no pilot

ductwork a system of passages used in heating, cooling, and ventilation to deliver and remove air

efficient well organized and works well

electrical grid the network of power plants, transmission lines, substations, and distribution lines that deliver electricity from power stations to homes and businesses

ember a glowing piece of wood or coal from a fire

engines machines designed to convert forms of energy into mechanical energy

environmental footprint the impact a person, organization, or activity has on the environment

erecting putting up

erosion the wearing away and moving of soil, rock, or other materials by natural forces including water, wind, or ice

evaporates turns from a liquid into a vapor

evolving developing gradually from a simple to a more complex form

feats achievements that took great courage, strength, or skill

fiber a long, threadlike part of a plant

flexible able to bend

fossil fuels energy sources, including coal, oil, and natural gas, that were formed when prehistoric plants and animals died and were buried by layers of rock. Fossil fuels are nonrenewable

friction the resistance that one surface encounters when moving over another

furnace an enclosed structure in which material can be heated to very high temperatures

fuse box an electrical panel used to distribute electricity through homes

generation creation of something

geysers natural hot springs

global climate the average climate of the world

gravitational forces the forces that pull objects with mass toward each other

harnessing controlling and making use of something

helium a colorless, odorless gas

helix a three-dimensional (3-D) spiral that curves around an axis

hydroelectric describes electricity made by the power of moving water

hydrogen a colorless, odorless gas that can be used to generate electricity

implement to put something into effect

Industrial Revolution a period of major economic and technological change that began in the eighteenth century in Europe and then spread to North America

ingenious smart, original, and inventive

innovation implementing ideas to create something new

inventors people who devise a new process, appliance, or machine

kinetic energy the energy of motion. Any object that is moving has kinetic energy

lasers very narrow beams of light
low-voltage electrical energy that is below a certain voltage, usually between 50 and 1,000 volts
marine related to the ocean
mechanical energy the energy an object has as a result of its motion or position
mining extracting, or taking out, valuable minerals and materials from the earth
offshore drilling drilling into the ocean floor to access the oil and gas that lie beneath the ocean floor
oil refineries facilities that process crude oil, coal, or natural gas into fuel and other products
optimize to make the best or most effective use of something
parasites organisms that live on or inside other organisms, called hosts. Parasites get their food from their hosts
particles minute portions of matter
penstock a channel or pipe that controls water flow or delivers the water to hydroelectric systems
pioneers the first people to do something
pollutes contaminates with harmful or poisonous substances
portable can be moved to where needed
power outage a break in the supply of power, such as electricity, often caused by storms
predict to forecast what is likely to happen
primitive describes something that is very basic or unsophisticated
prototype the first version or device from which others are developed
reactors devices that produce and control the release of energy from splitting the atoms of certain elements
reflective capable of reflecting light or other radiation
renewable describes a source of energy that is not deleted by use. Renewable sources include water, wind, and solar
reservoir a large, enclosed body of water that is kept in reserve for use during times when water is not easily available
resourceful able to find quick and smart ways to overcome difficulties
revolutionized changed something drastically
robots machines that can do specific tasks with little or no human intervention
runoff the water that flows over and away from a surface
rural relating to the countryside
sensors devices that detect or measure things in the environment
shaft a long, narrow passageway
software computer programs
supercharged to greatly increase the power of something
sustainable able to be maintained at a certain rate or level
thong a leather strip
tides the alternate rising and falling of the surface of the ocean
timber wood
transparent can be seen through
tsunami a series of waves caused by the displacement of a large volume of water
urban related to cities and towns
viable capable of working successfully
water currents the continuous movement of water in oceans, lakes, and rivers, in a specific direction

FIND OUT MORE

Books

Furgang, Adam. *Energy Solutions for All* (Spotlight on Global Issues). Rosen Young Adult, 2022.

Hardyman, Robyn. *Solar Power* (Energy Evolutions). Cheriton Children's Books, 2022.

McCauley, Paula. *Engineering for Teens: A Beginner Book for Aspiring Engineers*. Callisto Teens, 2021.

Websites

Find out about brand-new innovations from the US Department of Energy (DoE) at:
www.energy.gov/topics/energy-earthshots-initiative

Discover resources and lots of games to learn more about the different fields in engineering at:
https://tryengineering.org

Read *A young person's guide to sustainable energy* at:
www.unicef.org/lac/media/40516/file/A-young-persons-guide-to-sustainable-energy.pdf

Publisher's note to educators and parents:
All the websites featured above have been carefully reviewed to ensure that they are suitable for students. However, many websites change often, and we cannot guarantee that a site's future contents will continue to meet our high standards of educational value. Please be advised that students should be closely monitored whenever they access the Internet.

INDEX

ABOUT THE AUTHORS

Sarah Eason and Cathleen Small have written a wide variety of books for teens, including many STEM titles.